The Practical Guide to Better Depositions

Examples and Commentary

Mark D. McCurdy & Suellen Wideman

Mark D. McCurdy & Suellen Wideman

Border Press
PO Box 3124
Sewanee, Tennessee 37375

borderpress@gmail.com

ISBN: 978-1-7346802-9-4

Printed in the United States

Table of Contents

About This Guide vi

I. Set-Up Questions 1

Example 1

Commentary 2

Contrasting Vignette 6

Commentary – Contrasting Vignette 7

II. "Starting" a Deposition 10

Example 10

Commentary 11

Contrasting Vignette 12

Commentary 12

III. The Funnel Technique 14

Example 15

Commentary 17

Contrasting Vignette 21

Commentary – Contrasting Vignette 21

IV. Follow-Up 23

Example 23

Commentary 25

Contrasting Vignette 29

Commentary – Contrasting Vignette 30

V. Asking Questions about a Conversation 32

Example 32

Commentary 36

Contrasting Vignette 39

Commentary – Contrasting Vignette 40

VI. Authenticating a Document – Timing & Tactics 42

Example 42

Commentary 44

Contrasting Vignette 48

Commentary – Contrasting Vignette 49

VII. Asking Questions about a Document 50

Example 50

Commentary 55

Contrasting Vignette 58

Commentary – Contrasting Vignette 59

VIII. Leading Questions for Seeking Admissions 60

Example 61

Commentary 63

Contrasting Vignette 66

Commentary – Contrasting Vignette 68

IX. Making Objections at a Deposition 71

Example 72

Commentary 73

Contrasting Vignette 76

Commentary – Contrasting Vignette 77

X. Handling Obstreperous Defenders 79

Example 79

Commentary 82

Contrasting Vignette 88

Commentary – Contrasting Vignette 89

About the Authors 91

Mark D. McCurdy 91

Suellen Wideman 92

About This Guide

The genesis of this Guide is found in our Anatomy of a Deposition Program. Recently, a participating attorney expressed a desire for a source that could be consulted beforehand that would also serve as an ongoing resource after the program.

This Guide evolved into a stand-alone resource. Broadly speaking, it covers four areas: (1) how to control the record (Sections I and II); (2) learning everything the witness knows (Sections III-VII); (3) locking it all in (Section VIII); and (4) making and dealing with objections (Sections IX and X). Each section reflects best practices based – not on academia – but on our years of practical experience. Each is a strong example of how to accomplish the goals set out at the start of each section. The accompanying commentary sections memorably explain the thinking behind the questions. Understanding the "why" behind the example empowers you to improve your style and better your depositions.

The Guide takes on ten unnecessarily problematic areas where lawyers often struggle. The first two of these are at the very start of the deposition. There is tension between Section I's terse, quasi-leading questions that yield an unequivocal record for later use in motions and trials and Section II's more conversational style used to learn information, our primary deposition goal. The two examples show how to maintain balance on this tightrope.

Sections III and IV cover information-gathering skills necessary for learning at any deposition. Example IV reflects our view that good follow-up skills are the heart of the deposition process. Sections V through VII apply the general skillset to two specific areas that commonly occur in deposition practice. Section V details how to ask questions about a conversation and Sections VI and VII provide organizing principles for authenticating and asking questions about documents. All of the sections are brought home in Section VIII where the key tools for translating learning into admissions are detailed.

The contrasting vignettes in each section illustrate the hazards that stem from failure to embrace the example demonstrated in the transcript. These vignettes are designed to be realistic, but bad. A review of their defects becomes a compelling argument for the use of the example language.

Please note that Example II is actually a continuation of Example I, separated for analysis and discussion. Similarly, Examples V through VIII are related. Example V, which is about a conversation, uncovers a document that is authenticated in VI, the subject of questioning in VII, and used for the basis of the admissions in VIII. Examples III and IV are stand-alone, as are the final two examples.

Finally, in the transcripts, T means taking lawyer, and D means defending lawyer. As to the "Q" and "A," we think you've got that.

Mark & Suellen

I. Set-Up Questions

Goals: Tone; record protection

Key Methods
Close off escape routes, don't close off the witness; separate the set-up from the substance.

The opening segment of your deposition is more important than you may think. It is your chance to: (1) lock in key testimony for motions and trial; and (2) close off the witness' typical escape routes when in a pinch at trial. To accomplish these twin goals, focus at the start of the deposition on politely "taking away the life preservers" or escape routes that the witness grasps for if they change their story at trial and are being impeached. The art of the exercise is to accomplish these goals without shutting down the witness' willingness to talk.

Example 1, below, artfully locks in the testimony without intimidating or Mirandizing the witness making them afraid to answer questions fully.

Example – Set-Up Questions

Taking lawyer [T] – Introduce yourself to opposing counsel, witness, and court reporter. Give the reporter the case caption, business card, then ask to be alerted if any answer is not audible. The court reporter will appreciate your also providing a list of names and technical terms that are likely to be used in the deposition. Ask the court reporter to swear the witness.

acknowledging oath

T: Mr. Schmidt, my name is ____________ and I will be asking a series of questions regarding your claim for a breach of contract related to an information technology – or "IT" – vulnerability study for the

Woodall & Marcus Brokerage. Before we do that, do you understand that you are under oath?

A: Yes.

Q: Do you understand that this means you are swearing that all your answers to my questions are true and correct?

A: Yes

understanding process

Q: If at any time you do not understand any question I ask you, will you let me know?

A: Yes.

Q: If at any time during this deposition you realize that an answer you gave earlier is not correct or complete, will you let me know?

A: Yes.

Q: I will arrange for a short break every hour or hour and a half. Are you comfortable with that?

A: Yes.

capacity

Q: Is there any reason at all why you would not be able to give full and complete testimony today?

A: No, unless you tell a joke.

Q: Please just answer my question. Is there any reason at all why you would not be able to give full and complete testimony today?

A: No.

transition

Q: I'd like to start with some background information. Please tell me about *[comfortable topic]*.

Commentary

A strong sequence of initial set-up questions locks down testimony and eliminates escape routes - without harming tone. These questions communicate to the witness, and therefore to the fact finder and jury, the important circumstances of sworn deposition testimony. They are posed in a way that does not threaten the witness, and in an order that is designed to lessen their impact on the rest of the deposition.

Wall off the rules portion from the rest of the deposition.

Avoid blending the explanation of the rules of the deposition with questioning substance. It yields a cleaner transcript. To wall-off the rules/set-up portion from the rest of deposition. the attorney briefly explains the areas that will be covered but and says "[b]efore we do that, do you understand that you are under oath." This beginning starts the separation of the fairly lawyerish, not especially conversational set-up questions from the questions that follow. The last question does the same. In the last question the attorney transitions by saying, "I'd like to start with some background information. Please tell me about [comfortable topic]." For more information on this topic, see Section II, "Starting" a Deposition (p. 10).

Lock the witness in.

After a beginning question, the attorney starts to lock in the witness' answers in the remainder of the deposition. The key questions are:

Q: Do you understand that you are under oath?

Q: Do you understand that this means you are swearing that all your answers to my questions are true and correct?

Use this exact question - our favorite:

Q: If at any time you do not understand any question I ask you, will you let me know?

When answered with a "yes," the deponent is taking on an affirmative duty to tell you if a question is not understood – eliminating later claims of misunderstanding.

The attorney used an elegant wrap-up question that you may want to use with a deponent:

> Q: Is there any reason why you would not be able to give full and complete testimony today?

If you have a specific reason to ask questions regarding use of drugs or alcohol, use the following questions:

> Q: Have you taken any drugs that would interfere with your ability to remember the events of this case? *[If so, postpone deposition.]*
>
> Q: Have you taken any drugs that would interfere with your ability to testify truthfully about the events of this case? *[If so, postpone deposition.]*
>
> Q: Have you been drinking alcohol? *[If so, get details.]*

These questions are "off-putting," and should only be used when there is an objective basis for concern. Otherwise skip them.

Politely take away their life preservers.

When witnesses testify differently at trial from what they testified at deposition, they are subject to impeachment during cross-examination. To avoid looking un-credible, witnesses grasp at various life preservers in an attempt to explain contrary deposition testimony. The most common of these are that, at the deposition, "I did not understand your question," "I was not feeling well," or "I was confused." The questions and answers in Example I leave the witness without these common explanations for any inconsistencies.

All the questions focus on that mission. If a question does not remove a life preserver, cut it. Do not: (1) note the presence of opposing counsel; (2) discuss the role of objections; or (3) instruct the witness that answers must be verbal. Save these instructions for later use only if those situations occur. Otherwise, you are simply reminding the witness of the serious consequences and formal nature of the deposition process and shutting the witness down.

Tone is important.

The challenge is to create a useful record for impeachment without harming your relationship with the witness. You are, after all, making a first impression. Your attitude at the start of the deposition reflects that of a lawyer helpfully instructing the witness on the rules of the game. You are in reality walking a tightrope between forcing the witness to acknowledge the gravity of the testimony and at the same time encouraging the witness to speak freely in response to your questions.

Less experienced takers tend to veer towards an overly friendly tone, or an overtly prosecutorial one. This example shows it can be done if you are careful in word choice and execution. This is consistent with our definition of a good deposition: it feels like a conversation, yet it reads as a precise interview.

Get the answer you deserve.

On a smaller note, the vignette demonstrates the subtle control that the examiner has at the deposition. Note this exchange:

Q: Is there any reason at all why you would not be able to give full and complete testimony today?

A: No, unless you tell a joke.

Q: Please just answer my question. Is there any reason at all why you would not be able to give full and complete testimony today?

A: No.

When a witness does not answer your question, you should insist on a proper response. Be careful to get the answer you deserve. The first response was not as useful as the second would be in an impeachment.

Please see the contrasting vignette that follows for a questioning style that we discourage.

> **Key Takeaways**:
> Separate **rules** from **substance**
> Take away **life preservers** (confusion, memory, capacity)
> Keep tone **neutral and non-threatening**

Contrasting Vignette – Set-Up

Q: Mr. Schmidt, you understand you're under oath, right?

A: Yes.

Q: And you know you can't lie?

A: Yes.

Q: And if you do, that's perjury?

A: Yes.

Q: And you understand I'll be asking you questions about this contract?

A: OK.

Q: And I will need you to answer verbally. Nods of the head are not enough for the court reporter creating this transcript.

A: OK.

Q: And your attorney may, from time to time, make objections. I will usually ask you to respond to my questions despite those objections, unless they involve privilege.

A: OK.

Q: And do you understand that you may take a break at any time, unless there's a question pending?

A: Yes.

Q: Have you been drinking alcohol today?

A: Absolutely not. It's 10 a.m.!
Q: And are you taking any drugs?
D: Objection. You are harassing the witness.
A: That's none of your business.

Commentary – Contrasting Vignette – Set-Up

This harsh set of questions makes the deponent wary and shortens answers. The attorney also fails to politely "take away the life preservers," and unnecessarily reminds the witness of the formality of the proceedings and the presence of opposing counsel into the set-up questions. Finally, we also see in the vignette, the problem of verbal tics.

Rather than explaining the rules of the deposition helpfully as was done in the first example, this vignette is threatening and off-putting. It mentions lies, perjury, accuses the person of morning drinking, and pries into the deponent's medical history. Threats kill candor. Moreover, if used at trial, such treatment of the witness may make the jurors uncomfortable.

Not taking away their key life preservers.

The single most commonly-grasped-at life preserver "I did not understand your question" remains available to the witness, as does the tried and true excuse of "I was not feeling well." Only the understanding of the oath was acknowledged.

Do not inject formality or the opposing counsel's presence into the set-up questions.

In the contrasting vignette, the taking lawyer uses three set-up questions that do not focus on locking in testimony for impeachment uses at trial. There is absolutely nothing wrong with these instructions, but each is unnecessary at this point in the deposition.

Here, as part of the set-up questions, the lawyer says:

Q: And I will need you to answer verbally. Nods of the head are not enough for the court reporter creating this transcript.

Wait until the witness responds to a question with a nod or shrug to say you need the witness to answer "out loud." Doing so prematurely is a reminder to the witness of the seriousness and formality of the deposition process. This may lead to more measured responses than you want and lessen how much you learn at the deposition.

The vignette's next question only heightens the message that the witness should be careful. In it, the attorney actually reminds the witness that the witness has an attorney.

Q: And your attorney may, from time to time make objections. I will usually ask you to respond to my questions despite those objections, unless they involve privilege.

This is not the type of question that builds rapport or encourages expansive answers. It is the functional equivalent of "you know your lawyer is watching you right?" It encourages limited rather than expansive answers. If and when the attorney makes an objection during the deposition you can state this on the record, but it does not need to be in your set-up questions.

Finally, the contrasting vignette has an instruction on breaks that veers towards losing control of your deposition. The deposing lawyer asks:

Q: And do you understand that you may take a break at any time, unless there's a question pending?

Contrast that with this question from Example I:

Q: I will arrange for a short break every hour or hour and a half. Are you comfortable with that?

While polite, the first one empowers the witness to decide when breaks are taken. The second keeps the timing of breaks firmly in the taking lawyer's hands.

In sum, streamline your set-up questions to focus on those that enhance an impeachment at trial, and avoid questions that only serve to inhibit the witness by reminders of the formality of the deposition process.

Recognize and deal with your verbal tics.

The questions also reveal a common conversational tic that is often carried into deposition practice. In this case, the lawyer's tic is the word "and." These "ands" dilute the usefulness of the deposition transcript – any one of them cannot form the basis for an effective impeachment. The fact that the question starts with "and" will make its context questionable.

Curing this problem requires first, self-awareness. Once you become aware of a verbal tic ("and," "OK," echoes, etc.) write the word in easily seen letters at the top of your outline or even on a sticky note. Then frame the word with the universal no symbol. You will be surprised how well this works.

Common Mistakes to Avoid:

Being aggressive in tone or words in set-up questions
Intermingling set-up questions with facts of case
Questions that remind witness of the presence and power of their attorney

II. "Starting" a Deposition

Goal: Get the witness talking

Key Methods
Shift from control to curiosity; train early; silence invites talking

Set-up questions train the witness to give short answers. The tight transcript in Section I undercuts the atmosphere necessary for learning the witness' "whole truth." In Example II, below, which flows immediately from Example I (p. 1), details how to retrain the witness to give longer answers.

In the title of this section, "starting" is in quotes. The deposition actually began earlier, as soon as the witness was sworn. However, this stage of the deposition should feel like the start to the witness. Done well, it helps the witness relax and give expansive answers.

Example – Questions for "Starting" a Deposition.

Q: I'd like to start with some background information. Please tell me about your education.
A: Everything?
Q: Let's start with high school. When did you graduate from high school?
A: 2002.
Q: What high school?
A: Kokomo High School.
Q: What did you do next?
A: I went to college at the University of Notre Dame.
Q: When was that?
A: The Fall of 2002.
Q: What did you major in?

A: Drama.

Q: Really? That's fascinating. What made you pick Drama as a major?

A: I've wanted to be an actor from the time I was a young man. My mother did some amateur theater and it was so exciting. I got to play the part of one of the children in the "King and I" when I was eight – and I was hooked.

Q: How important is acting in your life now?

A: It's an outlet. I still act in local theater from time to time.

Commentary

Set-up questions train the witness to give short answers; this section begins retraining the witness to answer more expansively. Generally speaking, we take depositions to get the witness to talk to learn about their view of the case. In Example II, the questioning lawyer easily slides into a more conversational open-ended questioning style, beginning with the transition phrase, *"I'd like to start with* some background information."

Knowing that people generally enjoy talking about themselves, the transition in this case is to educational background. It is comfortable for both the witness and the attorney. While responses remain somewhat guarded at first, when the lawyer shows interest, you have this exchange:

> Q: What did you major in?
>
> A: Drama.
>
> Q: Really? That's fascinating. What made you pick Drama as a major?
>
> A: I've wanted to be an actor from the time I was a young man. My mother did some amateur theater and it was so exciting. I got to play the part of one

of the children in "The King and I" when I was eight – and I was hooked.

The great comedian George Burns once attributed his success to his "sincerity." The lawyer's apparent interest in the witness' choice of drama as a major, opens the witness up. Early time invested in getting the witness to talk pays great dividends later in the information-gathering phase of the deposition.

Please see the contrasting vignette that follows for a questioning style that we discourage.

Key Takeaways:
Make the transition from tight → open questions
Show curiosity, resist the urge to control
Early tone determines later answers

Contrasting Vignette – "Starting" a Deposition

Q: Okay. Let's talk about your background. You went to college, correct?
A: Yes.
Q: And you graduated?
A: Yes.
Q: Did you get a degree?
A: Yes.
Q: What was your major?
A: Drama.
Q: So you're trained to act?
D: Objection. Argumentative.

Commentary – Contrasting Vignette – "Starting" a Deposition

In this contrasting vignette, the lawyer neglects to make the transition to a more conversational mode. This lawyer is not gathering information; instead, the lawyer is engaging in cross-examination.

While it is acceptable to lead a witness through background information, that type of exchange is not rapport-building. Generally it should be avoided. Questions calling for single-syllable answers do not encourage a witness to relax, or indeed, even to talk. This questioning style teaches the witness to give short answers, not expansive ones. When the deposition goal is to obtain information, this attorney's adversarial manner is counterproductive.

Key contrast.

In Example II, silence and curiosity encourage narrative responses. Here, what may be an effort to control the witness appears aggressive to the witness, discouraging longer responses.

Common Mistakes to Avoid:
Too many leading questions
Rushing into substance
Sounding too lawyerish, scripted, or insincere

III. The Funnel Technique
Information gathering

Goals: General to specific; learning and confirming

Key Methods
Get the list before working the list; "what else?" > "Anything else?" Don't move on too early.

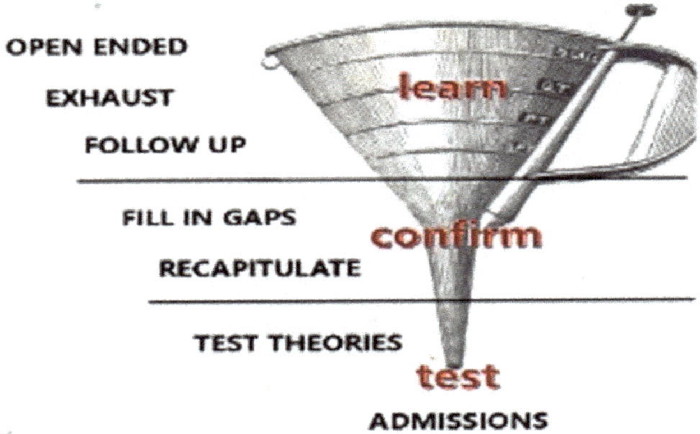

Now that the witness is talking, apply the funnel technique to learn and confirm what the witness knows. The funnel technique is a well-established name for a widely used method of organizing topics, thoughts, and questions. It is a platform that disciplines you to obtain information, exhaust the topic, and analyze the answers with follow-up questions.

Because the funnel technique lends itself to complete coverage of an area, it is particularly useful when employed as a guide for deposition questioning. Moving from the general to the specific, as shown below in Example III, the funnel technique allows the questioner to satisfy the three main goals of every deposition:

learning new information; confirming information obtained from other sources; and evaluating how good a witness the deponent would make at trial.

Example – Questions for the Funnel Technique

T: Ms. Panne, I want to talk to you now about what you saw when you first boarded the ship.

A: OK.

open-ended question

Q: Please describe what you saw when you first boarded the ship?

A: Well, it was about 25 feet long, the paint was in poor condition and when I boarded the ship, I noticed the engine cover was off.

exhaustion questions

Q: What else did you notice besides the peeling paint and the engine cover being off?

A: I noticed that one of the lifeboats was missing.

Q: What else did you notice about the condition of the ship?

A: Nothing else.

follow-up questions

Q: What do you mean when you say the paint was in poor condition?

A: It was peeling. There were big bare spots.

Q: Where?

A: At the water line, near the bow. On the left, I think it's called the port side of the ship.

Q: Anywhere else?

A: No.

Q: You also told me that you noticed one of the lifeboats was missing. How did you know that?

A: I saw the empty pulleys where the boat should be.

fill-in gap questions

Q: Was there anything you noticed about the instrument panel?

A: Oh yeah, now that you mention it. I noticed the ship's broken compass.

Q: What do you mean broken?

A: The cover was off and the little ball thing was hanging by a wire.

Q: What else did you notice about the ship?

A: Nothing.

recapitulation (or sum-up) questions

Q: Let me make sure I have this all. When you boarded, you noticed that the paint was peeling?

A: Yes.

Q: When you boarded, you noticed the engine cover was off?

A: Yes.

Q: When you boarded, you noticed the lifeboat was missing?

A: Yes.

Q: When you boarded, you noticed the compass was broken?

A: Yes.

Q: Have you told me everything you noticed about the ship when you boarded it that day?

A. Well, there was one other thing I wondered about.

Q: What was that?

A: There was a red sticker on the bow that read, "Unsafe - Failed Inspection - U.S. Coast Guard."

Q: What else?

A: That's everything.

Q: When did you first notice the red sticker on the bow?

A: As I walked up the gangplank to board the ship.
Q: What did you do after you saw that?
A: It gave me pause at first, but the tour had been recommended so I thought it was ok.
Q: What steps did you take to make sure it was ok?
A: I asked the mate about it. He said that it was an old sticker.

[continue with this line of inquiry to find out why the witness stayed on the ship.]

Commentary

Here, we see the funnel technique's full force as a questioning technique to learn and confirm. It illustrates six key steps:

(1) open-ended questions ("Describe …);
(2) exhaustion questions ("What else?);
(3) follow-up skills (break conclusions into facts);
(4) confirmatory questions (targeted prompts);
(5) tight summary questions (confirm the learning); and
(6) the strong use of lock-in questions to make sure the learning is complete.

Critically, always follow this sequence. Skipping any step will cost you information.

Learn.

The technique starts with broad open-ended questions on a selected topic. Here the topic was the condition of the ship used in an outing. The opening question was, "Please describe what you saw when you first boarded the ship?" Other good starting questions can begin with "explain" or even "tell me."

Get the list, work the list.

The questioner does not immediately follow up on the three observations given in the answer to the broad question. This is not a failure. It is a key point in properly employing the funnel technique. After the answer to the broad question, the next question should be an exhaustion question to probe deeper into the witness' memory. The question was:

Q: *What else* did you notice besides the peeling paint and the engine cover being off?

When the witness thought of another item, showing that memory had not yet been exhausted the next question was:

Q: What else did you notice about the condition of the ship?

"What else" should be one of the most frequent questions used during a deposition. It often yields more information. Moreover, use it before following up because it is difficult to remember to go back and ask, "what else?" later. Get the list before working the list.

As a side note, "anything else," a variation of this question, gives the witness permission to stop trying to recall more, and should not be used if you are trying to learn the witness' story.

Follow-up.

Having apparently exhausted the witness' memory, the taking lawyer was ready to begin following up. Follow-up is critical and is detailed in the next section (Section IV, p. 23).

Use follow-up to turn conclusions and generalizations (the natural language of the witness) into verifiable facts. In this example, the initial observation was that the "paint was in poor condition." "Poor condition" is a conclusion. Hence the taking lawyer's follow-up questions:

Q: What do you mean when you say the paint was in poor condition?
A: It was peeling. There were big bare spots.
Q: Where?
A: At the water line, near the bow. On the left, I think it's called the port side of the ship.
Q: Anywhere else?
A: No.

These simple but critical questions translate the phrase "poor conditions" into factual assertions that can be checked. Follow-up questions are the heart and soul of the deposition process.

Confirming.

After spending the bulk of the example following up on the information learned, the taking lawyer shifted gears to the confirming portion of the funnel technique by employing fill-in-the-gap questions. Fill-in-the-gap questions are targeted questions based on facts you think you know but that the witness has not yet disclosed or recalled.

Confirmatory questions, being further down the funnel, are generally narrower in form. Here the initial confirmatory question was:

Q: Was there anything you noticed about the instrument panel?

"Did you," as in "did you see" something is often used in this stage. If the question yields a yes response, then a new fact is confirmed and follow-up on that response will likely be needed. If the witness says no, then the learning in the chosen subject matter appears complete.

But things often are not as they appear, so the funnel technique includes a final step in the confirmation section. That step requires recapitulating or summing up what you think you have learned and asking the witness if that is correct. Here the sum-up question was a series of one-fact questions starting with:

> Q: Let me make sure I have this all. When you boarded, you noticed that the paint was peeling?

After obtaining verification of all the new facts, the lawyer then astutely finished the area by asking a lock-in question:

> Q: Have you told me everything you noticed about the ship when you boarded it that day?

The hoped-for answer here was, of course, "yes I have." That would indicate complete coverage of the witness' observations when she first boarded the ship. It would have foreclosed the witness from remembering new information at trial. Instead, as it sometimes does, having all the information about what was seen outlined in a quick series of questions yielded a new response that requires more follow-up and, ultimately, another sum-up question.

Mastering the funnel technique allows you to achieve the "learn and confirm" goals of the deposition. Misused, you will not get a complete understanding of the witness' knowledge. The flaws attendant to bad questioning are revealed in the short contrasting vignette that follows. It shows a questioning style we discourage.

Key Takeaways:

From general to narrow questions
Get the list → then work the list
"What else" > "Anything else"

Contrasting Vignette – Funnel Technique

T: Ms. Panne, I want to talk to you about what you saw when you first boarded the ship. What did you notice?

A: Well, it was about 25 feet long, the paint was in poor condition, and when I boarded the ship, I noticed the engine cover was off.

Q: OK. And what else did you notice?

A: One of the lifeboats was missing.

Q: All right. Anything else?

A: No.

Q: OK. Let's move on to what happened after you boarded.

Commentary – Contrasting Vignette – Funnel Technique

The taking lawyer in this contrasting example made a number of mistakes. First, the attorney used "anything else" questions and got less information. Second, the lawyer quickly accepted the "no" answer to the "anything else" question without moving into the follow-up or confirmation portion of the funnel. Lost in the follow-up are important questions translating the witness' conclusions into verifiable facts.

Finally, it is seldom a good deposition strategy to hide what you know and have the witness react for the first time at trial. Here the taking lawyer would have known of problems with the instrument panel yet fails to ask the confirmatory questions. This is consistent with the overall tenor of the vignette. The taking lawyer moves too quickly, fails to follow-up, and does not lock in the answers. As a result, the most damaging fact to the plaintiff's case – the sticker about the failed Coast Guard inspection – is never mentioned, explored, or explained.

Common Mistakes to Avoid:
Working the list before getting the complete list (following up before exhausting the topic)
Asking "anything else" instead of "what else"
Forgetting that silence invites talking (especially with eye contact)

IV. Follow-Up

Goal: turn conclusions into facts

Key Methods
Follow-up turns words into evidence; interesting ≠ responsive – get both; understand before moving-on

Section IV below, continues the deposition about the witness' observations on boarding the ship with an emphasis on strong follow-up skills - the heart and soul of the deposition process. Strong follow-up skills strip away the gloss a witness may put over the facts.

Example – Follow-Up Questions

Q: When you boarded the ship, how many people were on board?

evasion

A: Doesn't matter – not many.
Q: What do you mean by "not many?"
A: Less than a dozen at that point.
Q: Who did you speak with when you first boarded the ship?
Q: Who did you speak with when you first boarded the ship?

disconnect

A: Well, I did not speak with the Captain at that time. He seemed preoccupied.
Q: What made you believe the Captain was preoccupied?
A: He was talking with a crew member and didn't even look up when I said good morning.
Q: You said good morning to him?
A: Yes.

Q: Any other interaction with the Captain when you first boarded the ship?

tone

A: No, *[with anger]* frankly, he was dismissive of me.

Q: Why did you characterize the Captain as "dismissive" of you when you first boarded the ship?

A: Like I said before, he didn't even look at me.

Q: Anything else lead you to feel he was dismissive of you?

timing

A: *[pause]* No.

Q: Are you sure there was nothing else? You seemed to hesitate with that.

A: It's just that he was rude – and I hate rude.

Q: What was your reaction to him seeming preoccupied and dismissive?

A: It made me mad. I paid a lot of money for the trip. I'd expect more attention.

Q: You said in response to my original question that you did not speak with the Captain "at that time." Did you speak with him at a later time that morning?

A: Not that morning. I did – when the storm started.

Q: We'll get to that in a few minutes but right now I'm focused on when you first boarded the ship. Did you speak with the Captain beyond saying good morning when you first boarded?

A: No.

Q: Who did you have a conversation with among the passengers?

word choice

A: I did not have a "conversation" with any of them.

Q: You seemed uncomfortable with the word "conversation." Why?

A: I traded eye rolls with one of the other guests, but that's not really a conversation.

Q: Thank you. Let me rephrase then. What interactions did you have with the other passengers when you first boarded the ship?

Commentary

Follow-up is an unnecessarily challenging skill for some deposers. To excel, turn vague answers, generalizations, and conclusions into verifiable facts. When the answer is a conclusion, follow-up prompts us to ask, "What do you mean?" When the answer is an opinion, follow-up prompts us to ask, "Why?" When the answer is vague, follow-up prompts us to ask, "What are the details?"

Despite its simplicity, doing this is challenging because, understandably, at the start of your deposition career you are focused on asking the next good question. Follow-up skills, however, require you to stop focusing on your next question and to listen actively to the deponent's response.

The example demonstrates the challenge of follow up with the first question:

Q: When you boarded the ship, how many people were on board?

A: Doesn't matter – not many.

Q: What do you mean by "not many?"

A: Less than a dozen at that point.

The witness' first response is initially dismissive and followed by a generalization, "not many." The taking lawyer stays on track and follows up in a classic style, asking what the witness meant by the generalization "not many." The next response is "less than a dozen." The lawyer mistakenly accepts the answer instead of asking for the exact number.

Unravel the conclusions.

The remainder of the example demonstrates strong follow-up skills. This reflects hard work by the deposing lawyer. Note the number of follow-up questions (pp. 23-25) that were necessary just to deal with the question and witness' statement that:

Q: Any other interaction with the Captain when you first boarded the ship?

A: No, [*with anger*] frankly, he was dismissive of me.

At least four additional questions were used to unwind the conclusory language that the Captain was "dismissive."

Employ active listening.

Active listening requires paying rapt attention to the witness' words and tone – all while also analyzing the non-verbal body language of the witness.

In addition to listening for generalizations and conclusory words, the transcript shows five other specific areas deposing attorneys must be sensitive to when taking a deposition. The five are:

(1) evasion (no answer);
(2) tone (anger, sarcasm);
(3) timing (pauses);
(4) disconnects (non-answers); and
(5) word choice (outside the expected).

Evasion.

Example IV does a good job of follow-up when the witness appears to evade the question.

Q: When you boarded the ship, how many people were on board?

A: Doesn't matter – not many.

Q: What do you mean by "not many?"

The lawyer does not get distracted by the off-handed "it doesn't matter" comment. Instead, the lawyer stays focused on learning how many people were on the ship when the witness boarded. Often, repeating the question allows you to not be sidetracked by the attempted distraction thrown out by the evasive witness.

Timing.

When a witness is slow to answer what seems to be a simple question, candor becomes a great follow-up tool.

Q: Anything else lead you to feel he was dismissive of you?

A: *[pause]* No.

Q: Are you sure there was nothing else? You seemed to hesitate with that.

A: It's just that he was rude – and I hate rude.

As this example shows, follow-up up skills depend on listening skills. After the lawyer picked up on the witness' struggle, follow-up was easy.

Tone.

Observing that the witness seems angered by the Captain's apparent dismissiveness, the lawyer used this follow-up:

A: No, *[with anger]* frankly, he was dismissive of me.

Q: Why do you characterize the Captain as "dismissive" of you when you first boarded the ship?

A: Like I said before, he didn't even look at me.

Q: Anything else lead you to feel he was dismissive of you?

A: No.

Alternatively, candor could be used again. You can imagine saying to a witness, "You seem angry; are you?" or "You sounded sarcastic; did you intend to be?" This is a form of follow-up that often allows a witness to let go of the anger and focus on answering your questions.

Disconnects.

A disconnect occurs when a good question yields an intriguing response *that does not respond to* the good question. Your interest in the intriguing response may trigger your follow-up skills, but first ensure that the deponent answers your original good question.

Q: Who did you speak with when you first boarded the ship?

A: Well, I did not speak with the Captain at that time.

The witness' answer identified someone the witness did *not* speak with, i.e., the Captain. Remaining unanswered is the original question about whom the witness *did* speak with. The lawyer persists:

Q: You said in response to my original question that you did not speak with the Captain "at that time." Did you speak with him at a later time that morning?

When the witness says no, the lawyer again returns to the question of whom the witness spoke with, asking:

Q: Who did you have a conversation with among the passengers?

As we now know, the witness did not speak with anyone, but exchanged eye rolls with another passenger. This comes about only because the lawyer recognized the disconnect.

Word choice.

The witness' responses are filled with thoughtful word choices. Let's focus on the final one concerning the word "conversation:"

Q: Who did you have a conversation with among the passengers?

A: I did not have a "conversation" with any of them.

Here the lawyer picked up on the witness' "air quotes" around the word "conversation." Candor was then used, the issue was resolved, and the question was improved:

Q: You seemed uncomfortable with the word "conversation." Why?

A: I traded eye rolls with one of the other guests, but that's not really a conversation.

Q: Thank you. Let me rephrase then. What interactions did you have with the other passengers when you first boarded the ship?

By paying attention to the word choice, the lawyer was able to resolve the language issue.

Final thoughts.

Fundamentally, good listening skills involve your ears, your eyes, and your gut. Do not move on from an area until you understand the witness' response – and can prove or disprove it.

Please see the contrasting vignette that follows for a questioning style that fails to do necessary follow-up.

Key Takeaways:
Turn conclusions and generalizations into verifiable facts
Listen more stop standing ahead to your next questions
Stay until you **understand can prove**

Contrasting Vignette – Follow-Up

Q: When you boarded the ship, how many people were on board?

A: Not many.

Q: What do you mean by "not many"?

A: Less than a dozen.
Q: Who did you speak with?
A: Well, I did not speak with the Captain at that time. He seemed preoccupied and frankly dismissive of me.
Q: Okay. Did you speak with any passengers?
A: I did not have a conversation with any of them.
Q: All right. Let's talk about the condition of the ship. Ms. Panne, when you boarded the ship, the paint was peeling, correct?
A: Yes.
Q: The engine cover was off?
A: Yes.
Q: One of the lifeboats was missing?
A: Yes.
Q: So, you knew the ship was unsafe when you boarded it, didn't you?
D: Objection. Calls for a legal conclusion.
Q: You may respond.
A: No. I was confident all issues would be resolved before we left port.

Commentary – Contrasting Vignette – Follow-Up

This vignette shows the information that is lost when strong follow-up skills are not employed. Notice the information lost in this simple exchange:

Q: Who did you speak with?
A: Well, I did not speak with the Captain at that time. He seemed preoccupied and frankly dismissive of me.
Q: Okay. Did you speak with any passengers?
A: I did not have a conversation with any of them.

Lost, because of the lack of follow-up, is the chance to learn who was spoken to, what was said, and whether instructions or warnings were given.

Overall, comparing Example IV (p. 22) to the contrasting vignette yields two key points. First, the good example isolates word choice and gently probes it. This vignette allows the apparent evasion to pass unchallenged.

Second, admissions come *after* learning, not instead of it. The vignette reveals the perils associated with premature admission seeking.

> Q: So you knew the ship was unsafe when you boarded it, didn't you?
>
> D: Objection. Calls for a legal conclusion.
>
> Q: You may respond.
>
> A: No. I was confident all issues would be resolved before we left port.

The taking lawyer failed to exhaust facts first, gave the defense an easy objection, and missed the chance to build a stronger foundation for the admission.

Common Mistakes to Avoid:
Accepting conclusions without breaking them into facts Ignoring ambiguous language ("usually," "generally") Focusing on the next question instead of listening to the answer

V. Asking Questions about a Conversation

Goals: exhaustion; memory flood; write the movie

Key Methods
If you can't "film it," you aren't done; avoid summaries – get the words; exhaust before moving on

While Sections I-IV build a general skillset for learning and confirming the witness' story, attorneys may struggle when it comes to specific areas such as conversations. This is because they do not have short, memorable organizational techniques assuring complete coverage. In Sections V-VII, we provide such techniques. This is a critically important deposition skill. Conversations occur in almost every setting and will pop up in almost every deposition.

The cardinal rule of depositions regarding conversations is to use the deposition to reconstruct the conversation and resist any witness' attempts to summarize it.

These next three sections arise from a claimed breach of contract action involving an IT vulnerability study. The issue was whether a contract had been formed. Example V details the implementation of a five-step, film-based conversational model detailed in the commentary that follows. Examples VI and VII cover how to deal with documents disclosed in the deposition about the conversation.

Example – Questions for Conversations

Q: What was the next step in your effort to obtain a contract with Mr. Woodall and Ms. Marcus?

A: A face-to-face meeting.

Q: When did you meet with Mr. Woodall and Ms. Marcus?

A: February 18.

setting

Q: I want to turn now to that meeting on February 18. Where did the meeting take place?

A: In their 16th Street office.

Q: Where particularly in the 16th Street office?

A: Ms. Marcus' office.

Q: Please describe the room setting.

A: Her office had a desk and then a seating area. We sat in the seating area around a coffee table.

length

Q: How long was the conversation?

A: About 10 minutes.

cast

Q: Who was there?

A: An assistant or aide of some type. I didn't catch the name.

Q: Describe the assistant to me please.

A: Sure. She was a younger woman, likely in her 20's.

Q: Where did she sit?

A: Beside the desk, behind Ms. Marcus.

Q: What role did the assistant play in the conversation?

A: None that I noticed.

Q: Were you, Ms. Marcus, Mr. Woodall, and the assistant the only people in the room during the conversation?

A: Yes.

dialogue

Q: How did the meeting start?

A: I wouldn't call it a meeting; it was just a conversation.

Q: How did the conversation start?

A: Ms. Marcus initiated it.

Q: What did she say?

A: She thanked me for coming in, said she had heard good things about my IT skills, and wanted to see if we could do business together.

Q: What did you say?

A: I thanked her and asked her what kind of work she was looking for me to do.

Q: How did she respond?

A: She described a security project she wanted me to do. She explained that the brokerage had been hacked over the weekend, and while the system was back up, she needed an IT vulnerability study, and she needed it quick.

Q: What was said next?

A: We talked about how fast I could get to the project and what type of premium I would charge to give it my immediate attention.

Q: What exactly did you say?

A: I can't give you the exact words.

Q: Please do the best you can.

A: I told them I had a number of on-going projects requiring my attention, but that if necessary, I could see if those clients could give me a bit more time. If they would, I could prioritize theirs, charging essentially time and a half my normal fee since weekends and evenings would be necessary.

Q: What was the reaction?

A: She indicated that was reasonable.

Q: Were those the words used, that your time and a half premium was "reasonable"?

A: Not exactly.

Q: What were the exact words.

A: It was more of a nod of agreement.

Q: Any words accompanying this nod?

A: No.

Q: Was anything else discussed at the meeting in Ms. Marcus' office on February 18 in addition to the vulnerability study and the contract price terms?

A: No, I don't think so.

Q: Please think about it. I want to know everything that you and Ms. Marcus talked about. In addition to the vulnerability study and the contract terms you just explained, what else did you and Ms. Marcus discuss at the 10-minute meeting in her office on February 18?

A: *[pausing]* Nothing else.

Q: Are you sure?

A: Yes.

Q: Have you told me everything you can remember about the February 18 conversation with Mr. Woodall and Ms. Marcus?

A: That's all I can recall.

other resources

Q: Were any notes taken at the meeting?

A: Not by me. The assistant was taking notes for them.

Q: Was the conversation recorded in any fashion?

A: Not that I am aware of.

Q: Did you talk with anyone later about the conversation?

A: No.

Q: Did you ever see any notes, from the assistant or anyone else about the February 18 conversation in her office?

A: No.

Q: Did you ever see anything in writing about the conversation?

A: Just the alert letter I wrote to the subcontractors.

Commentary

When a conversation takes place between the parties (before the litigation), complete exhaustion of the topic is vital. This matters because Federal Rule of Evidence 801(d)(2) turns these statements into admissions. To ensure the necessary complete coverage, we lean on a 5-step model illustrated in the deposition and explained below.

The five-step, film-based conversational model.

With the stakes so high, it is important to develop a repeatable model for dealing with conversations. Our five-step model analogizes the deposition about a conversation to the creation of a movie about the conversation. This serves the goal of reconstructing the conversation because, to turn the testimony into a film, we need special emphasis on these elements:

Step 1 - When and where the conversation took place (the setting for the film)?;

Step 2 - How long the conversation lasted (the length of the movie)?;

Step 3 - Who was there (the cast)?;

Step 4 - What was said (the dialogue)?; and

Step 5 - What confirms that (search for other resources)?

Example V follows the model. First, the meeting place and time are established (Step 1 - the setting). Note the level of detail in the questions as to place, which includes the question:

Q: Describe the room setting for me.

This question seeks to take the witness' thoughts back "into the scene" by asking for a description of the atmosphere. We refer to this technique as "memory flood." It enhances the witness' ability to recall the details of the conversation with more accuracy.

Having transported the witness back to the setting of the conversation, the next question is about the length of the conversation (Step 2 - length). Knowing the length gives you an idea of how much time you should spend on it – we intuitively know that more is said in a 30-minute "contract formation" conversation than in one that lasts only ten minutes.

The question then turns to participants and other witnesses to the conversation (Step 3 - the cast). Before asking about the details of the conversation, check for witnesses (even if the conversation was by phone). Here there were apparently two silent witnesses who may have different recollections of the conversation.

Having established the set, length, and cast, the lawyer then moves to the heart of the issue, the words of the conversation (Step 4 - dialogue). Note how this is done:

Q: How did the conversation start?

A: Ms. Marcus initiated it.

Q: What did she say?

Move chronologically through the conversation, breaking the dialogue into increments. The questions in Example V followed a consistent pattern:

Q: What did she say?

Q: How did you respond?

Q: What was said next?

Seek facts, not characterizations. For example, the witness was not asked if the parties had reached an agreement. This examination is about what was said, not what the witness believed. Having the words of the conversation will allow the lawyer to undercut any later, and potentially false, characterizations of the conversation.

It is helpful to avoid "big bite" questions. The witness was not asked for a broad characterization of the conversation with a question like "what was the substance of the conversation?" Instead, true to our model, the first question was "how did it start."

Many deposition questions about conversations end with Step 4's exhaustion of the dialogue but Example V does not. Instead, it segues into a search for other resources to confirm information, Step 5. Question whether any notes were made, if the conversation was recorded in any fashion, whether the conversation was discussed with others, and if any documents were generated as a result of the conversation. Finding there was a contemporaneous alert letter to the key subcontracting partners is a true gem and authenticating that letter and asking questions about that letter are discussed in the next two examples.

Exhaust the witness' memory of the conversation.

Exhausting a topic means learning all about the conversation that can be learned. Here it is accomplished with two questions:

Q: In addition to the vulnerability study and the contract terms you just explained, what else did you and Ms. Marcus discuss at the 10-minute meeting in her office on February 18?

Q: Have you told me everything you can remember about the February 18 conversation with Mr. Woodall and Ms. Marcus?

These questions, and the witness' response, exhaust the topic. Having said there is nothing else that he can remember, the witness' testimony is locked in.

Please see the contrasting vignette that follows for the problems that flow from an examination that fails to follow this five-step, film-based conversational model.

Key Takeaways:
If you can't "film it," you're not done Get words, not summaries Exhaust memory before moving on

Contrasting Vignette – Questions about a Conversation

Q: You met with Ms. Marcus about the project, right?
A: Yes.
Q: When was that?
A: On February 18, I believe.
Q: What in substance did you talk about?
A: The security project and payment terms.
Q: And you claim that she agreed to hire you?
A: Yes.
Q: When was the agreement reached?
A: At the meeting.
Q: You claim she said the premium was reasonable?
A: Yes.
Q: Okay. Anything else important?
A: No.
Q: All right.

Commentary – Contrasting Vignette – Questions about a Conversation.

The terse deposition questions set forth above may have an allure of efficiency but are inadequate for a good deposition. First, the taking attorney violates the cardinal rule of depositions about conversation by asking:

Q: What in substance did you talk about?

This question invites the witness to characterize the meeting, not reconstruct it.

Because of this and other conclusory questions, the transcript lacks usable quotations, follows no recognizable sequence, and gives no context or details about the conversation. It fails to lock in the words and therefore destroys any impeachment opportunities if the testimony should later change.

The example also fails because it resorts to leading questions at critical moments.

Q: So there was an agreement reached?

A: Yes.

Q: And she said the premium was reasonable?

A: Yes.

These questions do not elicit fact-based responses. They permit the witness to simply conclude – for reasons that are unexplored – that an agreement had been reached. This leaves the witness free to add information at trial without fear of impeachment.

In sum, this contrasting vignette fails because it promotes conclusions, leaves any corroborating material unexplored, and most critically, allows the witness to define what matters by asking conclusory questions.

Final thoughts.

Good questioning about a conversation uses the five-step, film-based conversational model to reconstruct and exhaust the conversation. Questions are kept in sequence, dialogue is built while separating speakers, and conclusions are avoided in favor of actual words spoken. These questions close the door to later additions or changes to the testimony. Finally, good questioning about a conversation includes a search for corroborative evidence before moving on to the next topic.

Common Mistakes to Avoid:
Inviting the witness to summarize the conversation
Ignoring time, place, and number of participants
Not identifying other resources regarding conversation

VI. Authenticating a Document – Timing & Tactics

Goals: Authentication; birth/life/death; recall v. recognition

Key Methods
strategize timing; build persuasive foundations; remember the transcript

In addition to conversations, a second area where lawyers struggle is with the use of documents at a deposition. Common problems are: (1) when and how to authenticate a document; and (2) what questions to ask about documents. Example VI, below, takes on the first problem – authentication.

Authenticating key documents is a good use of a deposition time, especially when the witness may be unavailable or hostile in court. It is also true when you anticipate having to argue hearsay exceptions (here past recollection recorded) and want a strong transcript to assist in any argument or motion.

The transcript that follows occurs immediately after Example V (p. 32) on asking questions about a conversation.

Example – Questions Authenticating a Document

timing

Q: Have you told me everything you recall about the meeting on February 18?

A: Yes.

Q: Do you know of any documents that resulted from the February 18 meeting?

A: What do you mean?

Q: For example, did you take any notes, write any letters or write anything down in any way?

A: Yes, I wrote an alert letter to two key members of my team.

Q: Anything else?

A: No.

Q: What do you mean by an alert letter?

A: A note telling them I had gotten this opportunity and asking them to confirm their availability.

Q: When did you write it?

A: That afternoon.

Q: And by "that afternoon" do you mean the afternoon of February 18?

A: Yes.

Q: Who are these key members of your team that you wrote the alert letter to?

A: Ms. Pearce and Mr. Lemmey.

Q: Both in one letter?

A: Yes.

persuasive foundation:

Q: Is February 18 the date you put on the letter to Mr. Lemmey and Ms. Pearce?

A: Yes.

Q: What did you write it on?

A: My consulting business letterhead.

Q: What is the name of your consulting business?

A: RiskLedger.

Q: How long was the letter?

A: Two pages I believe.

Q: Did you sign it?

A: Yes.

Q: Is there anything on the signature area in addition to your signature.

A: Yes – my name, followed by my title.

Q: What title do you use?

A: I am the President.

consider the record

Q: I am handing the witness what was pre-marked as Exhibit 17. It is a two-page document, Bates 110953SW with the letterhead RiskLedger that bears the date February 18, addressed to Mr. Lemmey and Ms. Pearce, and containing a signature line that reads "John J. Schmidt, President." Counsel, here is a copy. Mr. Schmidt please review it and let me know when you are finished.

A: I am done.

Q: What is Exhibit 17?

A: It is a copy of the alert letter we were just talking about.

Q: How do you know?

A: I wrote it, it has my signature, and I remember writing it.

Q: Is this a fair and accurate copy of the alert letter you wrote to Mr. Lemmey and Ms. Pearce on February 18?

A: Yes, it is.

Commentary

"Bullet-proofing" a key document provides assurance of its admissibility at trial and makes the exhibit useful in any impeachment opportunity during cross-examination. Doing this takes very little time out of your deposition. Doing it effectively requires adherence to three principles as well as an awareness of an important work-around for difficult witnesses. The three principles for authenticating a document are:

Principle One - ensure timing is a strategic decision;
Principle Two - build a persuasive foundation, not a minimal one; and
Principle Three - create a useful transcript with exhibit numbers and descriptive phrases.

Also, not illustrated in the example but discussed below, keep in mind that foundations can be built with leading questions to an uncooperative witness.

Exhibits shape answers.

At the outset of Example VI is a critical point that we want to make explicit. When given an exhibit, a witness will read it and almost always constrain their answers to the words in the exhibit. The critical point: exhibits shape answers.

Imagine, for example, that you want to know who attended a certain meeting. Marking and giving a witness a copy of the meeting minutes, with the first lines listing who was in attendance, will shape that testimony – the witness will likely read back the attendance listed in the minutes. If, as better practice, you ask the witness "who was there?" without showing the minutes, you are likely to get the "unshaped" memory of the witness, not a recitation of the minutes. Consider carefully when you first show an exhibit to a witness.

Recall vs. recognition.

To counter the fact that exhibits shape answers, first ask questions that seek the witness' (1) recall of the event, followed by (2) recognition of documents or facts related to the event. This method will get you the most information – you initially ask the witness about the event, probing their memory (i.e., recall). After the witness has exhausted memories of the event, show the relevant exhibit(s) to stimulate further memory (i.e., recognition).

At the very start of Example VI, you see use of recall before recognition. The first exchange was:

Q: Have you told me everything you recall about the meeting on February 18?

A: Yes.

In so doing, the lawyer first asked the witness to recall the events of February 18. Only after exploring the witness' recall does the attorney move to the "recognition" stage of the examination.

Build a persuasive foundation.

Once you decide the timing is right, Principle Two is to use the deposition to create a persuasive foundation and authenticate the exhibit. Under F.R.E. 901, authentication simply requires you "to produce evidence sufficient to support a finding that the item is what the proponent claims it is." To get the best results, however, construct a persuasive foundation.

Persuasive foundations are built with this key point in mind: when a document (or other exhibit) is given to the witness, the juror should already know exactly what it is and why this witness knows that. This can be accomplished at the deposition if you take the time to have the witness describe an exhibit before asking them to authenticate it. These questions include:

Q: Who did you write the alert letter to?

Q: Is February 18 the date you put on the letter?

Q: What did you write it on?

Q: How long was the letter?

Q: Did you sign it?

Q: Is there anything in addition to your signature.

Q: What title do you use?

With this descriptive questioning and answers, the persuasive foundation is being built.

Always consider the record.

Finally, after building a persuasive foundation, make a usable transcript. Using the answers you received at the disposition, you can state:

> I am handing the witness what was pre-marked as Exhibit 17. It is a two-page document, Bates 110953SW with the letterhead RiskLedger that bears the date February 18, addressed to Mr. Lemmey and Ms. Pearce, and containing a signature line that reads "John J. Schmidt, President."

This description of the exhibit does not have you testifying (a no-no in court). You are not, for example, saying that the exhibit is signed by the President. You are instead describing that the document contains a signature line that reads "John J. Schmidt, President."

You next give counsel a copy, ask the witness to review it, and then ask two additional questions:

Q: What is the document marked exhibit 17?

Q: How do you know?

The description of the document, using the words from the deponent, forces the witness to acknowledge that the document is the alert letter. As important, it also creates a clean, easily searchable transcript for the document.

A small but important point. The exhibit number is followed by the Bates number. In cases with multiple depositions, the exhibit numbers may change but, by immediately adding the Bates number, the record remains clear.

Leading questions are permissible.

When dealing with an uncooperative witness, shift to a controlled, leading-question-generated foundation:

Q: You wrote an alert letter.

Q: You wrote it on February 18.

Q: The alert letter you wrote was two pages long.
Q: You addressed it to both Mr. Lemmey and Ms. Pearce?
Q: You signed your name at the end.
Q: You added your title.
Q: Your title is President.

It is your deposition, you are in control, and if leading questions are necessary, feel free to employ them.

Please see the short contrasting vignette that follows for the hazards that can come from ignoring the power of the three principles.

> **Key Takeaways:**
> Timing matters → **exhibits shape answers**
> Use **recall → then recognition**
> Build a **persuasive foundation**, not minimal

Contrasting Vignette – Authenticating a Document

Q: I'm showing you what's been marked as Exhibit 17. Do you recognize it?
A: I'm not sure.
Q: Well, it's your February 18 letter, right?
A: It may be. It looks like something from my files.
Q: You sent this letter after the meeting, correct?
A: Can I take a minute to read it?
Q: Just assume it's the letter we've been talking about. That's your signature at the bottom?
A: It looks like it.
Q: Okay. Let's move on.

Commentary – Contrasting Vignette – Authenticating a Document

As short and perhaps familiar sounding as this contrasting vignette is, it contains major mistakes. First, no effort was made to learn the witness' recall of the letter. This error focused the witness on the document and thereby risked limiting memory to recognition. A lot of learning was lost here. Second, the questions that were asked were suggestive and imprecise. The poor questioning style culminates in the virtually useless exchange:

Q: Just assume it's the letter we've been talking about. That's your signature at the bottom?

A: It may be. It looks like something from my files.

Such a question does not advance the inquiry at all; it invites witness resistance and trial objections. The response, "looks like it" is not authentication.

Finally, the contrasting vignette is notable for what was not done. The taking lawyer never asks:

Q: How do you recognize it?

Q: Why did you write it?

Q: Is this a true and accurate copy?

Each of these omitted questions would have played an important role in authentication of the document.

The consequences flowing from such poor questioning in the contrasting vignette will be felt if the case goes to trial. The attempted foundation in the contrasting transcript was too equivocal to ensure the exhibit's admissibility.

> **Common Mistakes to Avoid:**
> Showing the document too early
> Getting recognition before recall
> Weak, checklist-style authentication

VII. Asking Questions about a Document

Goals: learn the "why;" make a useful

Key Methods
exhibits shape answers; use exhibit as springboard for what you don't know; explore birth/life/death of document

For the same fundamental reason that attorneys struggle with conversations, the lack of a memorable organizational system also causes many lawyers to struggle when asking questions about documents. Organizing those questions works best if you keep in mind the birth/life/death approach shown in Example VII below and explained in the commentary that follows.

Example – Questions about a Document

Q: I am handing the witness what was pre-marked as Exhibit 17. It is a two-page document, Bates 110953SW with the letterhead RiskLedger that bears the date February 18, addressed to Mr. Lemmey and Ms. Pearce, and containing a signature line that reads "John J. Schmidt, President." Counsel, here is a copy. Please review it and let me know when you are finished.

A: I am finished.

springboard

Q: What is Exhibit 17?

A: It is my alert letter of February 18 to my two key consultants informing them of the audit job I discussed with Mr. Woodall and Ms. Marcus.

Q: How do you know?

A: I recognize it, it is on my letterhead, and has my signature at the end.

Q: Who is Exhibit 17, the February 18 alert letter, addressed to?

A: Mr. Lemmey and Ms. Pearce.

birth

Q: Describe how you went about writing your February 18 alert letter.

A: From my memory of the conversation with the brokerage that I had just finished. I do that all the time.

Q: Were there any drafts of this letter before this one, Exhibit 17, went out?

A: No, I just sat down and knocked it out in one try.

Q: I note that Exhibit 17, the February 18 alert letter, begins by stating, "This letter is to alert you to an upcoming opportunity with a new client I garnered earlier today." Why did you feel a need to alert them?

A: I wanted to get on the radar of the firm of Lemmey and Pearce. This would have been a big audit in a short amount of time, and I would need both Mr. Lemmey and Ms. Pearce to get it done.

Q: Any other reason you wrote both of them?

A: No.

Q: What do you mean by "upcoming opportunity"?

A: The brokerage's agreement to hire RiskLedger to conduct an IT vulnerability study.

Q: In the second paragraph of Exhibit 17, the February 18 alert letter, you write that "the essential parts of the agreement are" and then you list three factors: "the accelerated date; anticipated length of performance; and audit parameters." Why did you label those the essential elements of the agreement?

A: They are the heart and soul of work, and I wanted to be clear on the scope.

Q: When you used in Exhibit 17 the phrase "essential elements," what did you mean?

A: The terms of my contract with the brokerage.

Q: Do those three elements reflect the elements you claim you negotiated in the meeting with Woodall and Marcus?

A: Yes.

Q: Were those all of the terms that you agreed to at the meeting?

A: Yes.

Q: Anything else?

A: No.

Q: Where in Exhibit 17, the February 18 alert letter, do you mention the price or value of the contract?

A: In the third paragraph, where I mention the expected payment would be $25-30,000.

Q: The exhibit, Exhibit 17, says, "After reviewing the scope of the work, I estimate the cost charged for this service will be in the range of $25-30,000"; is that right?

A: That is what it says.

Q: When did you conduct that "review" of the scope of the work that you note in paragraph 3 of Exhibit 17?

A: As I was writing the letter.

Q: The letter appears to end with your signature and title, was there anything else on the original?

A: No.

life

Q: How did you expect Mr. Lemmey and Ms. Pearce to respond to Exhibit 17, the February 18 alert letter?

A: With some kind of indication of their availability.

Q: Why didn't you ask them in Exhibit 17 to confirm their availability?

A: It never occurred to me. I had worked with them before.

Q: Did you receive a letter in response from either of them?

A: No, not a letter

Q: Did either Mr. Lemmey or Ms. Pearce respond by any other means?

A: Steve Lemmey texted me gifs of a letter and a thumbs up. That's it.

get answer you deserve

Q: You concluded from those gifs that Lemmey and Pearce were agreeing to do the work without written confirmation?

A: I didn't need it in writing.

Q: That was not my question. You concluded from the thumbs up and letter gifs that they agreed to do the work without written confirmation?

A: Yes.

more life

Q: What did you do with the original of Exhibit 17, the February 18 alert letter to Mr. Lemmey and Ms. Pearce?

A: I mailed it to them.

Q: Did you keep a copy of your February 18 alert letter?

A: Exhibit 17 is the copy.

Q: How do you know they got your letter?

A: I mailed it to the right address; it should have been delivered. Oh, and the gifs Mr. Lemmey texted.

Q: How was Exhibit 17, the February 18 alert letter, mailed?

A: I put a stamp on it and threw it in the mailbox.

Q: Was Exhibit 17, the February 18 alert letter, sent by certified mail?

A: No.

Q: What other way or ways was Exhibit 17, the February 18 alert letter, sent other than by regular mail?

A: I don't understand your question.

Q: Was a copy emailed?

A: No.

Q: What did you do to make sure Exhibit 17, your February 18 alert letter, was actually received?

A: No other steps.

Q: Did you treat Ms. Pearce's failure to respond as acceptance?

A: I suppose so. Besides, I figured Lemmey accepted on behalf of both partners.

death

Q: After you mailed the original, what did you do with the copy that has been marked as Exhibit 17.

A: I put it in my files.

Q: What do you mean by files?

A: I keep a hard copy of paper for each client or prospective client, and I keep a computer file too.

Q: Let's start with the paper file. Where is that kept?

A: In my office, I have a lateral file cabinet behind my desk.

Q: What is in your file for this project?

A: Any documents relating to the work for the brokerage.

Q: Describe those documents.

A: They could be anything, project thoughts, alert letters to others who would be involved in the project, things like that.

Commentary

Good deposition questions about a document seek the information not apparent in the document itself. They follow a strong organizational pattern and maintain transcript discipline.

Developing this organizational pattern is critical. Our organizational technique revolves around the birth, life, and death of the document.

Use the document as a springboard.

The document is the springboard for asking about the intent, meaning, and significance of wording. It also encompasses questioning about omissions, timing, transmission, and retention. These are the types of questions that cannot be answered just by reading the document.

Notice the fundamental reporter questions used in the example to get beyond the words in the document.

Q: *What* do you mean by "files?"

Q: *When* did you conduct that "review" of the scope of the work that you note in paragraph 3 of Ex 17?

Q: *How* did you expect Mr. Woodall and Ms. Marcus to respond to Exhibit 17, the February 18 alert letter?

Q: *Why* did you label those the essential elements of the agreement in Exhibit 17, your February 18 alert letter?

Good questioning also includes asking about what the document does *not* include. For example, here the questioning focuses on the missing acceptance line in the letter.

Q: Why didn't you ask them in Exhibit 17 to confirm their availability?

You know what the exhibit says, focus your questions on why it was written that way and what it doesn't say. Lawyers less familiar with the deposition process struggle with this concept. But it is true of the deposition as a whole. *Depositions are about learning new information, not repeating what you already know.* If you find yourself asking the witness to read a document into the record, stop. Ask instead, what does this document *not* tell me?

Birth, life, and death.

It is important to have an organizational structure in mind when you are asking questions about a document. After much thought, we landed on a structure that covers the "birth, life, and death" of an exhibit. The lawyer in Example VII started with the birth question by asking why it was written and how it was composed. In this section the lawyer also asked about prior drafts. These questions should always be asked, and any prior drafts reviewed.

The lawyer then shifted to the "life" of the document in this set of questions:

Q: What did you do with the original of Exhibit 17, the February 18 alert letter to Mr. Lemmey and Ms. Pearce?

A: I mailed it to them.

Q: Did you keep a copy of your February 18 alert letter?

A: Exhibit 17 is the copy.

Q: How do you know they got your letter?

A: I mailed it to the right address; it should have been delivered. Oh, and the gifs Mr. Lemmey texted.

Q: How was it mailed?

A: I put a stamp on it and threw it in the mailbox.

Next the taking lawyer moved to the "death" of the exhibit, i.e., to the recordkeeping habits of the deponent. The fundamental question is why did you retain a copy of this piece of paper, and where did you get it from? These questions included:

Q: After you mailed the original, what did you do with the copy that has been marked as Exhibit 17.

A: I put it in my files.

Q: What do you mean by files?

A: I keep a hard copy of paper for each client or prospective client, and I keep a computer file too.

Q: Let's start with the paper file. Where is that kept?

The line of inquiry often uncovers other relevant material. In the example, the deponent suggests the file may contain correspondence with other members of the audit team, potentially including a contemporaneous document helpful on the issue of whether a contract was reached in this case. Searching into the death of the document can uncover an archive of material in only a few deposition questions.

Birth, life, and death is a strong organizing principle, and the example mirrors its elements. Had the transcript continued, more time would have been spent on death, asking about the electronic file, access to the file, back up procedures, and last accessed date. Other questions could revolve around any meta data fields that might exist, shared drives, and cloud storage. In short, death can be a lengthy topic delving deep into the other side's document management process and procedures.

Maintain record discipline.

Finally, the example also demonstrates an important practice pointer by consistently referring to "Exhibit 17, the February 18 alert letter" in the questioning. This discipline yields a strong transcript. Too many times we fall into the trap of referring to the exhibit as "it." It is natural in the deposition setting, you and the deponent have "it" in your hands and understand what the questioning is about.

When you hear yourself at the deposition using the "it," think about changing that to a descriptive phrase like "Exhibit 17, the February 18 alert letter" so your record will be precise. This skill assists a summary judgment motion or an impeachment where you need the judge or juror to understand exactly which document was in the hands of the witness at the time of the questioning.

Please see the contrasting vignette below, demonstrating the problems that arise from a cavalier handling of documents.

> **Key Takeaways:**
> Use the document as a **springboard** to answer what it doesn't say
> Organize around the **birth/life/death** formula
> Maintain record discipline

Contrasting Vignette – Asking Questions about a Document

Q: I'm handing you Exhibit 17. Please read the first paragraph into the record.

A: "This letter is to alert you to an upcoming opportunity …"

Q: Thank you. Now read the second paragraph.

A: "The essential parts of the agreement are …."

Q: And the third paragraph?

A: "After reviewing the scope of the work …."

Q: So the letter says the cost charged would be $25-30,000, correct?

A: Yes.

Q: The letter speaks for itself, right?

D: Objection.
A: I suppose.
Q: And it says the essential elements are the accelerated date, anticipated length of performance, and audit parameters, correct?
A: Yes.
Q: And you signed it?
A: Yes.
Q: And you mailed it?
A: Yes.
Q: That's all I have.

Commentary – Contrasting Vignette – Asking Questions about a Document

The goal of every deposition is to learn the other side's position and information. In this contrasting vignette, every question confirms what the document says, and no new learning is achieved.

This failure to probe results in a record that is insufficient to support any impeachment of that testimony. Moreover, by failing to explore what didn't happen, the omissions in the document remain unaddressed and the witness has room to provide creative answers at trial.

Two other flaws are apparent and important. First, there is no inquiry into the recordkeeping process of the company (the death stage of the document in our model). Second, the transcript's repeated use of the term "it" instead of "Exhibit 17" will make it difficult (and awkward) to use any of these responses at trial.

Once lost, these opportunities cannot be recreated.

Common Mistakes to Avoid:
Not learning the birth/life/death of the document Prioritizing control over learning Forgetting the transcript is for trial

VIII. Leading Questions for Seeking Admissions

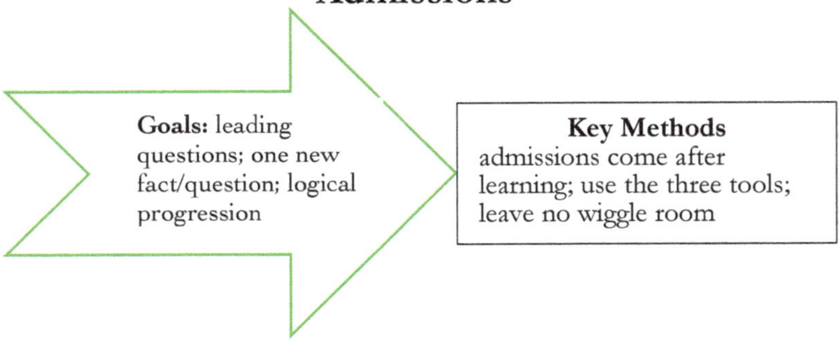

Everything that has occurred in the deposition up to this point is preparation for this section. The common situations for learning and confirming are covered in Sections III-VII. The time has come to focus on locking in the testimony and obtaining admissions.

Admission seeking is one of the most underused but powerful techniques in deposition practice. As noted previously (p. 36), under Federal Rule of Evidence 801(d)(2), admissions by a party opponent are defined as non-hearsay. Clean answers by a party opponent to crisp questions set the stage for enhanced motions for summary judgment and, in the rare case where the matter goes to trial, compelling opening statements and winning cross-examinations. Admission-seeking questions also help you gauge the settlement value of the case and evaluate the deponent's ability to withstand likely cross-examination.

Getting admissions requires a disciplined use of three tools. These tools are: (1) leading questions only; (2) one new fact per question; and (3) a logical progression to a specific goal. See how they are employed in Example

VIII below.

Example – Questions for Seeking Admissions

Q: You had a meeting with Mr. Woodall and Ms. Marcus on February 18?

A: It was a conversation.

Q: This conversation was at their office?

A: Yes.

Q: You discussed with them their brokerage's need for an IT vulnerability study?

A: Yes, a real rush job.

Q: You told them that a rush job would require overtime work?

A: I did, and it did.

Q: That overtime work required a premium fee?

A: Yes.

Q: That premium was 50% over your usual fee?

A: Yes.

Q: Ms. Marcus never said that the premium was acceptable?

A: She nodded in agreement.

Q: Ms. Marcus never told you in words that it was agreeable?

A: Not in words.

Q: Ms. Marcus never wrote to you that it was acceptable?

A: She did not.

Q: After this conversation you wrote an "alert" letter to two key subcontractors, Pearce and Lemmey?

A: Yes.

Q: They were your key personnel to complete the project in the 2-3 week time frame?

A: Yes, they were.

Q: You wrote that letter, Exhibit 17, because you

wanted to know if they were available for this project?

A: Correct.

Q: Mr. Lemmey did not confirm his availability for this engagement?

A: He sent a text that had gifs of a thumbs up and a letter that I took as confirmation.

Q: You did not receive any other confirmation from Mr. Lemmey?

A: That's true.

Q: Ms. Pearce did not confirm her availability for this engagement?

A: She did not formally confirm.

Q: You told them in Exhibit 17 that the price range was $25,000-$30,000?

A: It was an estimate, a range.

Q: The actual price you were going to charge for the project was not discussed with the brokerage?

A: Not formally.

Q: On February 18th, you thought the project would be going forward if you could get the subcontractors Lemmey and Pearce?

A: Yes.

Q: But you did not have their confirmation.

A: Not at that time.

Q: On February 18th, you thought the project would be going forward if you got the right price?

A: Of course.

Q: But you had not discussed the price with the brokerage.

A: Not at that time.

Commentary

This is the essential section of the deposition. To succeed in it, master the three tools when seeking admissions. First, you must structure tight leading questions. Second, these leading questions must contain only one new fact per question. Finally, the rhythm of the question must logically progress toward a specific and tightly focused goal. Let's look at each.

Leading questions only.

Leading questions are assertions, not suggestions. These assertions usually start with nouns, and seldom employ weak verb start questions.

In the example, the deponent is tenaciously asked almost exclusively leading questions.

Q: Ms. Marcus never said that the premium was acceptable?

A: **S**he nodded in agreement.

When the response to the leading question was equivocal, the attorney did not argue but simply repeated the question with a slight variation.

Q: Ms. Marcus never told you in words that it was agreeable?

A: Not in words.

Q: Ms. Marcus never wrote to you that it was acceptable?

A: She did not.

By maintaining form and focus, the sequence converted a witness' conclusion ("she nodded in agreement") into discrete and favorable facts (no words, no writing, only a gesture).

One new fact per question.

Second, the leading questions must be short and include only one new fact per question. This is actually two rules within one. First, and most critically, the questions must be fact-based. Violation of this part of the second rule is the most common reason theory testing fails. Here the taking lawyer asked:

Q: Mr. Lemmey did not confirm his availability for this engagement?

Q: Ms. Pearce did not confirm her availability for this engagement?

Q: Mr. Lemmey sent you a text that had gifs of a thumbs up and a letter?

Q: You did not receive any other confirmation?

By keeping the questions to one new fact per question, the witness had little room to maneuver. If instead the question contained an adverb such as:

Q: Mr. Lemmey did not *specifically* confirm his availability for this engagement?

or included a generalization such as:

Q: A picture of *silly gifs* was the *closest thing to a confirmation* you got, wasn't it?,

the odds increase that the witness will not agree with your assertion and the admission will not be obtained.

Notice too that even fact-based questioning is at risk of failure if the question combines more than one fact. Not asked, but illustrative of this phenomenon:

Q: She never said out loud that the premium was acceptable, she only nodded her head?

A: She did.

A reader will be left wondering whether Mr. Schmidt's response of "she did" meant that Ms. Pearce said the premium was acceptable, or whether it meant she "only nodded her head."

Logically progress to a specific goal – and stop.

Our third rule requires that the series of questions logically progress to a specific goal. Start with what you know, move toward what logically flows from that, and then move with confidence and in small steps toward what those facts mean (your theory).

The analogy is to climbing a ladder. Each rung you achieve advances the case, and even if you don't get to the top, you are likely to obtain acknowledgement of one or more helpful facts.

The example began with an ambiguity as to whether there was any acceptance of the proposed premium, next noted was the lack of confirmation of the two key subcontractors' availability, and closed with the fact that the total price had not been discussed. This led to the final exchange logically progressing toward the goal of proving that therefore was no "meeting of the minds" on February 18:

Q: On February 18th you thought the project would be going forward if you could get the subcontractors Lemmey and Pearce?

A: Yes.

Q: But you did not have their confirmation.

A: Not at that time.

Q: On February 18th you thought the project would be going forward if you got the right price?

A: Of course.

Q: But you had not discussed the price with the brokerage.

A: Not at that time.

"Not at that time" suggests that a discussion of price may have taken place later. Following up on this will not advance the theory that no contract was entered into during the February conversation between the parties. The lawyer wisely leaves it alone.

Final practice pointer.

Finally, one smaller but important point – do not sweat the little stuff. In this exchange the lawyer accepted the deponent's characterization of the events of February 18:

> Q: You had *a meeting* with Mr. Woodall and Ms. Marcus on February 18?
>
> A: It was a conversation.
>
> Q: This *conversation* was at their office?

The phrase meeting or conversation was not critical to the outcome at that point. For that reason, the lawyer accepted and used the word "conversation" but later changed back to the word "meeting," which the witness then accepted.

Please see the vignette that follows for an illustration of what happens when the lawyer does not follow the three rules for seeking admissions: leading questions only; one new fact per question; and logically progress to a specific goal.

> **Key Takeaways:**
> Use **tight leading questions**
> One new fact per question
> Logically progress to your goal – and stop

Contrasting Vignette – Leading Questions for Admission Seeking

Q: Why did you meet with Mr. Woodall and Ms. Marcus in the first place?

A: I was told it was about an IT penetration audit.

Q: And you wanted Pearce and Lemmey on the project, right?

A: Yes.

Q: Tell me everything that was discussed at that meeting.

A: We talked about the scope of the study and timing and some staffing issues.
Q: Did you talk about costs?
A: Yes.
Q: What did you say about cost?
A: I said it might require a premium because of the timing.
Q: But they never agreed to that, correct?
A: Well, Ms. Marcus nodded.
Q: So you are saying that she basically accepted the premium price?
A: I assumed so.
Q: And later that day you sent a letter about the project to a Mr. Lemmey and Ms. Pearce confirming everything?
A: Yes.
Q: Let me show you what was marked as Exhibit 17. Do you recognize it?
A: Yes.
Q: What is it?
A: A letter I sent after the meeting summarizing things to my subcontractors.
Q: And that accurately reflects what was discussed with the brokerage?
A: Generally, yes.
Q: And you had subcontractors lined up to help with that?
A: Yes.
Q: One of them was Mr. Lemmey?
A: Yes.
Q: And he agreed to be available?
A: He sent a text message with thumbs-up and letter gifs.
Q: So you took that as confirmation he was available?

A: Yes.

Q: Okay. I think that's all I have on that.

Commentary – Contrasting Vignette – Leading Questions for Admissions

This contrasting vignette demonstrates several common mistakes made in this area. These errors include: (1) carelessly using open-ended questions; (2) accepting characterizations from the witness and not translating them into "non-facts" (i.e., what did not happen); (3) arguing with the witness; (4) failing to convert ambiguity into admissions and (5) lacking a structure designed to persuade. Each of these errors is potentially fatal.

Open-ended questions.

The examiner repeatedly asks broad questions. For example:

> Q: Tell me everything that was discussed at that meeting.

This allows the witness to control the narrative and avoid clean admissions. The open-ended style risks answers that detour away from any point the taking attorney was trying to make.

Failure to clarify helpful conclusions.

Accepting characterizations, like the mistake of asking open-ended questions, forfeits control. It allows the witness to avoid facts and, instead, to interpret facts. Here the witness was allowed to characterize the exhibit as "generally" reflecting the discussions with the brokerage. The acceptance of the answer "generally" ruined any admission. It does not close off any later claims that the letter was inaccurate in part.

Do not become argumentative.

In contrast to the docile forfeiting of control pointed out above, the vignette also shows the importance of avoiding argument with the witness at this stage of the deposition. Arguments often force a deponent to "dig-in" and thereby avoid the admission. Argument also can, as we like to say, lead the witness in the wrong direction. In this case, the witness was questioned about his claim that he told them that overtime work would require a pricing premium. The lawyer then argued:

Q: So they never agreed to that, correct?
A: Well, Ms. Marcus nodded.
Q: So you are saying that she basically accepted the premium price?
A: I assumed so.

By arguing that the nod indicated acceptance, the lawyer led the deponent in the wrong direction. The better case is to isolate the nod as the only claim to acceptance, and not portray it as acknowledgment of any acceptance.

As a side note, questions that start with the word "so" tip your hand to the witness and counsel as potentially harmful to the witness before even another word is spoken. "So" avoid starting a question with the word "so."

The contrasting vignette lacks a structure designed to persuade.

The questioning lacks clear architecture. Rather than the logical progression illustrated in Example VIII, the above vignette jumps between topics. It hurdles between the original meeting with Woodall and Marcus, to the premium discussion to the exhibit and then to the interactions with the subcontractors. Lost in this shuffle is the underlying theme that the contract terms had not been fully worked out, resulting in the lack of an enforceable contract.

Final observations on admission seeking.

A deposition transcript becomes powerful not because the lawyer argues with the witness, but because the lawyer converts uncertain events into clear, discrete admissions. Strong admission-seeking questions isolate key facts, remove ambiguity, proceed in small steps, and leave conclusions for later argument.

Common Mistakes to Avoid:
Seeking admissions before learning and confirming the facts Asking open-ended, compound, or imprecise questions Leaving room for explanation

IX. Making Objections at a Deposition

Goals: leading questions; one new fact/question; logical progression

Key Methods
Pick your spots; let weak questions stay weak; be concise – don't argue

The first eight sections of the Guide focused on asking better questions at a deposition. Asking those questions will require you to deal with objections and handle occasional obstreperous defenders. Section IX focuses on the role of objections at the deposition, and is designed to make you a better deposition defender. Section X closes the Guide by providing tips for dealing with improper objections and the lawyers who make them.

Objections are the job of defending counsel and, done properly, protect both the record and the witness. In addition, objections can make a client more comfortable and alert and, therefore, a better witness. Example IX, below, proceeds from the same setting as Example III, (p. 15) (passengers going on a ship tour). It serves as an example of just how many objections can be made at a deposition.

The example details the objection's basis for clarity. In many jurisdictions, lawyers defending the deposition are limited to saying "objection" or "objection as to form." Rule number one for defending a deposition is to know the rules of the jurisdiction and adapt your objection style accordingly.

Example – Objections

Q: A few minutes ago, you said that you were mad at the Captain for not talking to you when you boarded the ship. Why were you mad?
D: Objection. Misstates prior testimony.
A: I never said I was mad.
Q: How would you characterize it then?
A: I just noticed he was preoccupied.
Q: What did he say or do?
D: Objection. Vague and ambiguous. Compound.
Q: What's vague about it?
D: Use of pronouns, vague as to time.
Q: *[to witness]* What did the Captain say or do on the day you boarded the ship that leads you to believe he was preoccupied?
D: Objection. Compound.
Q: You may answer.
A: He did not engage me and his expression was cross, like I had interrupted him.
Q: What had you interrupted?
D: Objection. Calls for speculation.
Q: What did you think you had interrupted the Captain from doing the day you conversed with him as you boarded the ship?
D: Objection. Misstates prior testimony.
A: I didn't have a conversation with him. I just tried to start one. He seemed to be having trouble with one of the crew who was working on the radio.
Q: So, as you boarded the ship that day, the Captain was working to make the ship safer, but you interrupted him?
D: Objection. Argumentative.
A: He refused to converse with me. If that is an interruption, so be it.

Q: Did you discuss this issue with anyone else?

D: Objection. Potentially privileged. I caution the witness not to divulge any of our conversations.

A: Other than counsel, no.

Commentary

Of course, in most circumstances, defending counsel will not object to every question. Defending attorneys must ask themselves: (1) can I object?; and (2) should I object (i.e., will it help my case/my client if I object)? Here there was no such introspective reasoning, instead the objections became a habit. Nonetheless, a review of the transcript shows that the objections were uniformly valid.

When must an objection be made? Understanding FRCP 30 and 32.

The most common question less-experienced deposition defenders ask is "when must I object?" A practical application of the rules requires limiting yourself to short nonargumentative, nonsuggestive objections (FRCP 30(c)(2)) if the question can be corrected at that time by the taking lawyer (FRCP 32(d)(3)(B). After an objection is made, the witness is to answer the question, and only if an attempt is made to use the transcript at trial will the judge make a ruling on the stated objection(s).

A classic example of this is a compound question. In the example, the taking lawyer asked:

Q: What did he say or do?

D: Objection. Vague and ambiguous. Compound.

The question is really two-fold. What did he say? What did he do? Because an objection would have allowed the taking attorney to correct the question by dividing it into two questions, it must be made at the deposition. If it is not, the answer can be used at trial despite the flawed compound question.

Most deposition objections follow this formula. If the question is flawed, and that flaw can be corrected (or, in our rubric, "fixed"), the defending lawyer must make the objection or forever hold his/her peace. Examples of questions that can be fixed are throughout the example, and each objection is valid and well placed. Notice how even a question that misstates prior testimony is correctable.

Q: A few minutes ago, you said that you were mad at the Captain for not talking to you when you boarded the ship. Why were you mad?

D: Objection. Misstates prior testimony.

It does indeed. The witness had said (see Example IV, p. 23) that the Captain was dismissive toward her, not that she was mad. The taking lawyer can fix the question.

You may validly make an objection to almost any question. Many questions for example, use pronouns or are indefinite in time. Take the question "what did he say?" Everyone in the deposition room may understand that question, but in isolation it is vague: who is the "he" and when did "he" say it. To avoid objections at a deposition, limit your use of pronouns and always "timestamp" your questions. The following chart shows the types of questions that courts deem correctable or "fixable."

These objections need to be made at the deposition to be preserved for court:

vague or ambiguous;	lacking a proper foundation;
compound;	argumentative;
misstate prior testimony;	asked and answered; and
misleading;	(sometimes) privileged.
speculative;	

Privilege is on this list because such an objection must be made at the deposition to prevent disclosure at the deposition. In that sense, an unmade privilege objection will result in an answer that thereby waives the privilege.

Questions that are not fixable do not need to be objected to at the deposition (but can be). If an attempt is made to use the transcript at trial, the objection can be made then. Non-fixable questions include questions that either concern or are:

- irrelevant;
- based on hearsay (unless an exception);
- offers of compromise;
- prejudicial;
- subsequent remedial measures;
- liability insurance; and
- the competence of the witness.

Objections to such questions may be made at the deposition if strategically appropriate of course (see below) but are not waived if not made at the deposition.

When should an otherwise valid objection be made?

Because so many objections are available, the issue for less-experienced lawyers is whether the objection is strategically merited. A flawed but meaningless background question about education may not be the type of question to which you would object.

In deciding whether and when to state an available objection, ask yourself two questions: First, would an objection help my witness/my case? Second, would an objection protect the record I want? If the answer to either of these questions is yes, then make the objection.

Some lawyers support a third question: can the objection be made without educating or improving the performance of the opposing counsel? If the end result of your objections is that the taking lawyer asks sharper questions, you have not helped your witness.

Key Takeaways:
Apply the "can I, should I" test
Know your rules
Do not coach

Contrasting Vignette – Making Objections at a Deposition

Q: When you boarded the ship, what did the Captain say to you?

D: Objection. Vague as to which boarding, vague as to which ship, vague as to time, lacks foundation, mischaracterizes prior testimony.

Q: The February 3, 2019, boarding we've been discussing.

D: Objection. You're assuming facts not in evidence about what we've been discussing. Also, argumentative.

A: He didn't really say anything.

Q: Did that upset you?

D: Objection. Calls for speculation about emotional state. The witness already testified she was not mad, and I object to the characterization. If you know, you can answer.

A: I wouldn't say upset.

Q: What was his facial expression?

D: Objection. Vague. Compound. Calls for speculation. You can answer if you know, but don't guess.

A: He looked irritated.

Q: Irritated with you?

D: Objection. Argumentative. Objection. Assumes facts not in evidence. Objection. Misstates testimony. She never said he was irritated with her.

Q: Did you talk to your lawyer about this event?

D: Objection. Attorney-Client privilege. I instruct the witness not to answer.

Q: I'm not asking what was said. I'm asking whether you discussed it.

D: Same objection. Do not answer.

Commentary – Contrasting Vignette – Objections at a Deposition

The vignette replicates three common errors in making objections at a deposition. These errors are: over-objecting to harmless questions; improper speaking objections that coach the witness; and the misuse of privilege. Let's examine each flaw.

The first is the common situation where a defending lawyer over-objects to a harmless question. In the vignette the witness was asked:

Q: When you boarded the ship, what did the Captain say to you?

This innocuous question was met with an objection listing five boilerplate grounds. As such it is excessive, distracting, likely to irritate the witness (as well as anyone later hearing the transcript) and most significantly, strategically pointless. The objection does not protect the record; it signals insecurity. Proper objections are not reflexive; they are thoughtful and intentional.

Second, the speaking objection made in response to the lawyer's question about the Captain not saying anything to the witness is improper and coaches the witness.

Q: Did that upset you?

D: Objection. Calls for speculation about emotional state. The witness already testified she was not mad, and I object to the characterization.

The defending lawyer's objection violates FRCP 30(c)(2) in that it is not stated "concisely and in a nonargumentative and nonsuggestive manner." The objection reminds the witness of prior testimony and signals the "right" answer. In so doing, the objection may result in sanctions in stricter jurisdictions.

Similarly, the objection telling the witness "you can

answer if you know, but don't guess" can be viewed as subtle coaching. It suggests uncertainty.

Finally, the vignette also abuses the attorney-client privilege and would be considered improper. It is another example of a reflex objection, here at least prematurely made. The question asked was:

Q: Did you talk to your lawyer about this event?

D: Objection. Attorney-client privilege. I instruct the witness not to answer.

Whether a communication occurred is generally not privileged. In situations such as this, the better response by the defending lawyer may be to go off the record and discuss the potential privilege with the taking lawyer. Another alternative is to state on the record, "Counsel, I know you do not want to invade the attorney-client privilege here. If you are asking whether we spoke, I would ask the witness to answer with a simple "yes" or "no."

In sum.

Every objection reveals strategy; excessive objections illustrate yours. If you can object at the deposition, ask yourself whether the objection would:

(1) help my witness?;

(2) protect the record the record I want?; or

(3) avoid educating opposing counsel?

If the answer to either of the first two is "yes," object. When you can also avoid educating opposing counsel by objecting, all the better.

Common Mistakes to Avoid:

Unnecessary objections that make your opponent better
Hesitating to make an objection
Making it personal
Coaching the witness

X. Handling Obstreperous Defenders

Goals: Diagnose behavior; escalate responses; build the record for court

Key Methods
stay calm; don't be pressured to rephrase; drive wedge between witness and lawyer

Properly made objections, as Example IX shows, are part of a deposition. However, some defending lawyers misuse objections. They try to throw you off your game or attempt to coach the witness. When this occurs, you must simultaneously diagnose their behavior and employ a series of escalating responses to get the behavior to stop.

In this example, from the deposition of defendant Ms. Marcus on the same topic as plaintiff Mr. Schmidt was asked about in Examples VI, p. 42, and VII, p. 50, we see how objections can be abusive and illustrate five responses to such objections. Each response is detailed further in the commentary that follows.

Example – Responses to Obstreperous Defenders

Q: When did you receive Mr. Schmidt's letter and what did you think when you read it.

D: Objection.

A: I got it next Monday, the 21st I think. It really irritated me because it was partial overreach.

step 1 - mentally review and, if appropriate, correct your question

Q: You read the letter that was marked as exhibit 17 on the next Monday, February 21?
A: Yes.
Q And you felt as you read it that it was a partial overreach?
A: Yes.
Q: Explain what you mean by partial overreach.
A: We had not fully reached an agreement yet. Cost was a big concern, and we wanted to see if another company could give us a better price than him.
Q: What steps did you take to find a lower price?
D: Objection.

step 2 – dismiss the objecting lawyer like a fly on the wall

Q: You may answer.
A: We called around to some other firms to see what they could do.
Q: Who did you call?
D: Objection.
Q: What is the basis of the objection counsel?
D: Misstates prior testimony.
Q: Are you instructing the witness not to answer?
D: No, I am not.
Q: You may answer.
A: Sterling Consulting and SWSolutions were the only ones we got through to.
Q: Were you able to find a better price?
D: Objection.

step 4 – slow the deposition

Q: What was the very first step you took to find a lower price
D: Objection.

Q: Counsel, this is the third consecutive objection you've lodged without any legal basis. The witness seems prepared to explain any steps that the brokerage was taking to obtain a lower price, and I am fully prepared to spend the next hour on those steps. It would be more efficient for all of us if we moved through this narrow area in less time. Ms. Marcus, what was the very first step you took to see if you could find a lower price.

A: We brainstormed other firms who could do the work and tried to contact them.

Q: Let's walk through that. What was the first firm you contacted?

D: Excuse me counsel while I consult with my client.

step 7 – carry and cite authority

Q: Unless you are consulting about a privilege, having a conference while my question is pending is generally improper. Here is a copy of our local federal rule for you to review. Please answer the question, Ms. Marcus.

A: We called SWSolutions.

Q: I'd like to return to something you mentioned earlier. You said you thought when reading Exhibit 17, the follow-up letter by Mr. Schmidt, that it was partial overreach.

D: Objection. She meant gross overreach.

step 8 – build a favorable record for court

Q: Court reporter, please mark the record. Counsel, that is not a proper objection. In fact it likely would be construed as a violation of FRCP 30(c)(2)'s admonition that objections must be stated concisely and in a nonsuggestive and nonargumentative manner. Ms. Marcus, did you say earlier that the letter was a "partial overreach?"

A I did, but I misspoke. It was a gross overreach.

Q: What made you change your testimony?

D: Counsel, I need to consult with my witness.

Q: This is the second time you've interrupted my deposition with an inappropriate conference while a question is pending. I again ask the court reporter to mark the record.

D: We are conferring.

Q: Let the record reflect that counsel is now whispering into the ear of the witness. This conduct, if it doesn't stop immediately, will force me to ask the judge to give up her time to review your behavior. I do not want to use the court's time in such a fashion, but I will if the behavior does not stop now.

D: Counsel, we will confer as we see fit.

Q: Court reporter, please again mark the record.

Commentary

Less experienced lawyers worry about a defender taking over the deposition and destroying the flow of their discovery and admission-seeking efforts. In our program, we detail ten steps for dealing with the range of inappropriate objectors. This example highlights five of our ten favorite escalating techniques:

Step 1 – mentally review and if appropriate correct your question;

Step 2 – dismiss the objecting lawyer like a fly on the wall;

Step 4 – slow the deposition;

Step 7 – carry and cite authority; and

Step 8 – make a favorable record for court.

Which techniques you employ depends upon the category of inappropriate objections you are dealing with.

Diagnose the behavior.

There are three common types of obstreperous defenders. The first is the "irritating lawyer." This species is notable for meaningless objections that do not harm the information flow. The second type is the "conferring lawyer." This is the type of lawyer who has frequent whispered conferences with their witness. Because you do not know the content of the conversation between the lawyer and the witness, this injects a concern that the information flow from the witness is unreliable. The final type of behavior is the so-called "testifying lawyer." This is the attorney who uses objections to signal to the witness the attorney's preferred answer to a pending question. This type of behavior can render a deposition useless, as you are not getting the witness' real answers.

All three behaviors are present in Example X, and dealing with each requires employing different strategies.

Step 1 – Ensure your question was good before escalating your response.

Objections are not all bad; sometimes, our questions may be unclear. That is why Step 1 is to check your question. This is done early on by the lawyer after the following exchange:

Q: When did you receive Mr. Schmidt's letter and what did you think when you read it?

D: Objection.

A: I got it next Monday, the 21st I think. It really irritated me because it was partial overreach.

The taking lawyer should know that the objection is valid because the question was compound. Here the dilemma is that the answer is also intriguing and potentially useful.

The witness says it was a "partial" overreach, a step back from the perceived defense that it was a total overreach.

The taking lawyer did not react to the objection. Instead, the lawyer cured the defect and preserved the answer by breaking down the question into its component parts:

Q: You read the letter that was marked as exhibit 17 on the next Monday, February 21?
A: Yes.
Q: And you felt as you read it that it was a partial overreach?
A: Yes.

The testimony is now admissible, and no more severe escalating tactics by the taking lawyer were necessary or appropriate.

Step 2 – Dismiss the objecting attorney like a fly on the wall.

The second tactic is to ignore the behavior and get it to stop. Do not engage as a matter of habit, but do signal to the defending counsel that their objections will not impede your legitimate deposition questions. Dismiss the objecting attorney like a fly on the wall, by ignoring the objection completely or politely telling the witness, "you may answer." This treatment makes the defending attorney look ineffective to the witness. It was illustrated in the following exchange:

Q: What steps did you take to find a lower price?
D: Objection.
Q: You may answer.
A: We called around to some other firms to see what they could do.
Q: Who did you call?
D: Objection.
Q: Are you instructing the witness not to answer?

D: No, I am not

Q: You may answer.

A: Sterling Consulting and SWSolutions were the only ones we got through to.

Step 4 – Slow the deposition.

Later in the transcript, however, the questions were valid yet nevertheless the objections continued. In this exchange, the lawyer escalated to Step 4 and slowed the deposition.

Q: Were you able to find a better price?

D: Objection.

Q: What was the very first step you took to find a lower price?

D: Objection.

Q: Counsel, this is the third consecutive objection you've lodged without any legal basis. The witness seems prepared to explain any steps that the brokerage was taking to obtain a lower price, and I am fully prepared to spend the next hour on those steps. It would be more efficient for all of us if we moved through this narrow area in less time.

Q: Ms. Marcus, what was the very first step you took to see if you could find a lower price?

These last two questions illustrate the escalation of the response, Step 4 in our progression. Note the form of the question – the lawyer first asks for the very *first* step taken to find a lower price. This wording signals that a long step-by-step inquiry is coming. This tactic, slowing the deposition in response to the objection, works well with the irritating lawyer. Teach the objecting lawyer that more objections yield more questions.

Step 7 – Carry and cite authority.

Ignoring the objection is not an option in the situation the taking lawyer next confronts when, while a question was pending, the defending lawyer consults with the deponent. The lawyer notes this:

Q: Unless you are consulting about a privilege, having a conference while my question is pending is generally improper. Here is a copy of our local federal rule for you to review. Please answer the question, Ms. Marcus.

A: We called SWSolutions.

Unless it relates to a privilege, consultations are generally while a question is pending. *See* applicable local federal or state rules in the jurisdiction of the case. The taking lawyer quickly called the defending counsel on the tactic and supplied a copy of the rule, making further conferences less likely. This demonstrates the importance of knowing your rules and carrying and citing authority.

Step 8 – Build a favorable record for court.

In some situations, against some counsel, no citation of rules or adjustments to your own behavior will stop the interference. Under these circumstances, build a record that will read favorably before a judge or magistrate if judicial intervention is necessary. This is Step 8 of our progression.

Getting a discovery dispute in front of the court must be viewed as a last resort for at least two reasons. First, going to court can take a long time. Second, any court matter can be lost. If court intervention is sought, you want to make clear that you are neither a bad actor nor rushing to court prematurely. Note these critical favorable record-building exchanges:

Q: Court reporter, please mark the record. Counsel, that is not a proper objection. In fact it likely would be construed as a violation of FRCP 30(c)(2)'s admonition that objections must be stated concisely and in a non-argumentative and nonsuggestive manner. Ms. Marcus, did you say earlier that the letter was a "partial overreach?"

Q: Counsel, this is the second time you've interrupted my deposition with an inappropriate conference while a question is pending. I again ask the court reporter to mark the record.

Each of these well-crafted comments by the lawyer is made to alert the opposing counsel that a favorable record is being made to take to court. The least subtle of those signals is the phrase "mark the record." As a practical matter, this is employed to allow easy retrieval of the sections involved should a hearing occur. As a tactical matter, "mark the record" sends a clear signal that you are considering judicial intervention.

Note also how the taking lawyer places the whispered conference on the record and states a reluctance to take the court's time.

Q: Let the record reflect that counsel is now whispering into the ear of the witness. This conduct, if it doesn't stop immediately, will force me to ask the judge to give up her time to review your behavior. I do not want to use the court's time in such a fashion, but I will if the behavior does not stop now.

Both actions are important steps, because if the conference was not detailed by the lawyer, it may not have been noted in the transcript. Second, it is clear that the taking lawyer respects the court's time.

Additionally, the comments escalate slowly into

harsher responses. In the first cited question, it is noted that the objection "likely would be" interpreted as violative of the rules. The second statement is firmer, but not personal and not judgmental. Only the third iteration portrays an aggressive manner. Escalation should be done slowly and professionally.

Final thoughts.

Relentless questioning and a good knowledge of the rules will stop most of this behavior before it escalates as it does in this somewhat apocalyptist example. But go into your deposition knowing your rules, carrying and ready to cite authority, and prepared to build a record that will make you look good if the matter requires judicial intervention. If you take these steps, you are likely to regain control of your deposition without having to involve the court.

> **Key Takeaways:**
> Maintain your **poise**
> Diagnose quickly, **escalate** slowly
> **Build a record** that elevates you – and not the dispute

Contrasting Vignette – Handling Obstreperous Defenders

Q: When did you receive Mr. Schmidt's letter?
D: Objection. Vague.
Q: That's not vague.
D: It is vague.
Q: Fine. When exactly did you receive the letter?
A: I don't remember.
Q: You just said it was Monday.
D: Objection. Misstates testimony.
Q: No it doesn't.
D: Yes it does.

Q: Counsel, this is ridiculous.
D: Ask a better question.
Q: Did you receive it on February 21?
D: Objection. Leading.
Q: It's a deposition. Of course it's leading.
D: Objection to form.
Q: Are you going to object to every question?
D: If they're improper.
Q: This is why nobody likes taking depositions with you.
D: That's inappropriate.
Q: Let's take a break.
[Off the record. 10-minute argument in hallway.]
[Back on record.]
Q: So where were we?
A: I'm not sure.
Q: Whatever. Let's move on.

Commentary – Contrasting Vignette – Handling Obstreperous Defenders

This contrasting vignette showcases four failures. First, instead of focusing on the witness, the lawyer spends the bulk of the time arguing with defense counsel. This argument escalates rapidly and turns emotional. As a result, the taking lawyer abandons the funnel approach and stops learning facts. It reflects a violation of a core principle: the deposition is about the witness, not the lawyer.

Second, by leaping towards escalation, the lawyer missed opportunities to defuse the situation. Note the taking attorney never asks, "what is the basis of the objection?" Instead, the taking lawyer assumes impropriety. Further, by not taking these simple steps, the lawyer loses the opportunity to diagnose the behavior and apply the appropriate escalating response. That is undisciplined.

Should the matter go to court, the record is inadequate to support judicial intervention. There are no sections of transcript marked, no rule citations mentioned, no measured warnings of the need to stop the behavior, and no structured escalation as in the proper example. This transcript would simply irritate most judges, and it is likely that neither party would receive relief.

Finally, and regretfully, here we see the inappropriate behavior actually succeeds. Notice the end point of the vignette:

Q: Whatever. Let's move on.

The bad conduct has triumphed.

Overall, the difference between the two vignettes is discipline. In the good example, the escalation is purposeful, a solid record is constructed, and the taking lawyer always keeps the witness at the center of the strategy. In this bad example, ego outweighs reason, no record is developed, and no learning occurs.

Common Mistakes to Avoid:

Failing to recognize the behavior
Rephrasing your question just because there's an objection (instead, consider, "you may answer")
Terminating the deposition
Failing to preserve key objections (form or privilege)

About the Authors

Mark D. McCurdy

Mark D. McCurdy is an award-winning teacher cited by a national advocacy skills provider for his "dedication to the art of advocacy." The proud father of Nathan and Tyler, Mark has taught advocacy skills since 1992.

He is the author of "Obtaining Admissions in Depositions," *Temple Law Review*, Volume 74:1 (Spring 2001). This l article, published in Temple's Symposium: Advocacy 2000, draws on Mark's extensive depositions experience in high profile matters. Together with Suellen Wideman and Sarah Reznek, he also authored *State v. Graves, a Telemarketing Fraud Prosecution Case File.* This case file is the basis for advocacy training by the National Association of Attorneys General. In 2021, again with Suellen Wideman, he wrote *Steal or No-Steal, Lessons for Litigators from February's Impeachment Proceedings.*

Mark served in the Maryland Attorney General's Office for almost 23 years, including a lengthy tenure in the Office's elite Civil Litigation division. He possesses an extensive trial and appellate litigation background. For over 3 years Mark served as the General Counsel for Maryland Automobile Insurance Fund ("MAIF"). In this role he oversaw and honed MAIF's legal representation throughout the Maryland judicial system, and practiced his persuasion skills on the Maryland General Assembly. In 2015, he was named Chief Executive Officer of this $200 million plus insurance entity.

Mark is a Phi Beta Kappa graduate of the University of Maryland College Park and holds a J.D. degree with honor from the University of Maryland Law School. He leads many deposition and trial training seminars, and lectures extensively across the United States on persuasion and communication skills for lawyers and law students.

Suellen Wideman

Suellen Wideman is an experienced trial and appellate attorney and a former Senior Assistant Attorney General in Maryland. In this role, she was involved with Maryland regulatory agencies that dealt with health care issues for more than 25 years, where she gave daily input into shaping Maryland's ever-evolving health care system. She had an important role in developing policies that sought to provide access to quality health care services for all residents of the state. She received the Jennifer Lauterbach Robbins Award for "her zealous advocacy in the public interest and for her willingness to litigate any issue with intensity, creativity, and perseverance."

Suellen successfully led Maryland's first prosecution for "unprofessional conduct in the practice of medicine" against an obstetrician/gynecologist who had "consensual" sexual relationships with patients. Other career highlights include defeating attacks on Maryland's regulatory framework for physician discipline and successfully defending the State's crucial expansion of cardiac surgery services in Maryland.

Teaching skills that she first sharpened as a public defender in Nashville, Tennessee, Suellen lectures extensively on all aspects of lawyering, including the expanding fields of fact investigation, negotiations, depositions, motions practice, supervisory skills, and trial advocacy. She is also the co-author of *State v. Graves, a Telemarketing Prosecution Case File,* which is used by the National Association of Attorneys General as a platform for advocacy training throughout the country. She led well over 100 advocacy skills programs for a national provider of legal skills training.

A native of Georgia, Suellen currently lives in Sewanee, Tennessee. She has an LL.M. from Yale Law School and a J.D. from the University of Tennessee College of Law.

www.ingramcontent.com/pod-product-compliance
Lightning Source LLC
LaVergne TN
LVHW050922210926
848482LV00012B/495
9781734680294